PAPIER MACHE

LONE HALSE

DAVID PORTEOUS
CHUDLEIGH DEVON

CONTENTS

INTRODUCTION

Papier mâché is a material that is both cheap to make and easy to work with. It is amazing the results you can achieve once you get started.

When we talk about papier mâché as a material for modelling, many people will probably think of the balloon-shaped piggy banks that most children try making at school, and often they don't think any further, and that is a shame!

I have had hours of pleasure working with papier mâché, and I am constantly astounded at how much scope the material presents. In the course of my work I have developed a number of techniques and designs, and I would like to share them with you in this book. After reading the book you will find that there is much more to papier mâché than just newspaper and paste. By using other materials you can produce, for example, bowls and figures that are so hard you would think they were made from clay or wood.

After making the models, you can take a long time over the actual decoration. There are lots of possibilities — you could use coloured paper torn into imaginative patterns or you could paint directly onto the various models, for example.

I have seen children in school making large figures out of papier mâché. These can be 2–3 metres (6–9 feet) high if they are built over a framework of wood and metal wire. If enough layers are used in the construction, they can even be strong enough to climb over.

This book does not deal with such large objects, but it will show you how to make a range of articles for decorative or everyday use to add colour to your daily lives.

Papier mâché will encourage you to use your creativity and to develop your own models. For this reason the book outlines a number of techniques that I hope will inspire and guide you. Once you have read these, you will be ready to start in earnest on your own.

Have fun!

Lone Halse

Lone Halse.

WHAT IS PAPIER MÂCHÉ?

The term papier mâché is of French origin and literally means 'chewed paper'.

It is so called because in some instructions for making papier mâché the paper is soaked in water until it becomes a soggy pulp.

Man has been acquainted with papier mâché ever since paper was invented, and it has been used in many forms for everyday and decorative purposes. In Venice in Italy, for example, the tradition of making masks out of papier mâché has lasted for centuries. The Chinese originally used it to make soldiers' helmets, but these days they use it to make large masks. In many other countries people have learned to make similar products out of papier mâché because it was cheap and easy to shape.

In Valencia in Spain a big folk festival is held every year, and the high point is when a procession of large papier mâché figures is carried through the town. The figures, which can be 3–4 metres (9–12 feet) high or more, stand on large lorries or are drawn by cars. When everyone has seen the procession, a vote is taken on which figure is the best. The winning figure is displayed in the centre of the town, and all the other figures are burned amid much public merry-making. It might seem strange to destroy several weeks' or months' work in a single moment, but it would be a hopeless task to keep all those huge figures year after year.

Nowadays we import a wide range of decorative objects made of papier mâché, most of which come from the East. In these countries the people sit outside in small villages and make imaginatively shaped animals out of papier mâché. This helps them to eke out a hand-to-mouth living. But when you see how little papier mâché figures cost in the shops, you realize just how small those amounts are. Some countries and regions are famous for producing special articles out of papier mâché. The people of Bali, for example, make extremely attractive masks in brilliant colours. These masks can be bought in decorative art shops in most parts of the world.

When people see the figures in the shops, you can guarantee that only a few will realize that the articles have been made from papier mâché. This is because the papier mâché has an extraordinarily robust surface and an extremely "solid" appearance. It is only when you lift a papier mâché article that you realize from its lightness that it is not made of wood or clay. It is a good idea to go hunting in the shops. If you really look carefully, you will find that the range of papier mâché goods available is greater than it has ever been. In some places you can buy small rocking-horses made from papier mâché. The good thing about coming across different types of article is that you can gain ideas and inspiration for your own models without having to copy.

Artists in the West have also begun to work with papier mâché as a form of expression. There are no limits to how large the figures can be if they are built up around a framework. Indeed, it is even possible to construct large-scale sculptures or monuments.

MATERIALS AND TOOLS

If you want to achieve a good result, it is important to use the correct tools and materials. This section briefly describes most of the equipment and materials you will need.

Card and corrugated card: These can be used for stiffening or to make templates or shapes.

Masking tape or paper tape: These are used for joining together parts of models.

Paper: Obviously this is indispensable. Old newspaper was used for most of the objects in this book, but you can also use ordinary white writing paper. Coloured paper can be used for decoration.

Brush: This is useful for brushing paste onto the paper. It can also be used for decorating.

Whisk: This should be used to make the paper pulp smooth and uniform.

General-purpose interior filler (such as Polyfilla): This is mixed with water and can be used to make the pulp mixture smoother and more resistant.

Scissors: These can be used for trimming edges and for cutting paper into pieces or into shapes.

Craft knife or scalpel: Use this when you want to cut the papier mâché.

Bucket or bowl: This is used for mixing up the papier mâché pulp.

Cold-water paste: This is as essential as the paper and is used in all the projects.

PREPARATION

In this section we shall be looking at the different types of papier mâché. We will begin with the most commonly known method, which involves tearing paper into pieces and gluing them with cold-water paste. The next section tells you about moulds and formers and how you should treat the different materials before you apply the pieces of paper.

TORN PAPER

You can use almost any sort of paper with this method. The most common type is old newspaper, which has the advantage of being cheap and relatively flexible to work with. Glue the paper with paste made from a mixture of water and powder stirred together. You can buy the paste at your local D-I-Y store, and it will tell you on the packet the proportions of water and powder to use. Be careful not to make the paste too thick or it will be difficult to work with. Equally, don't make the mixture so thin that it becomes "sloppy". You'll have to experiment a little!

If the mixture is too thin, you can always add a little more powder. If you find it is too thick, you will have to thin it out with water. When you stir the mixture, it is best to use a whisk or hand-mixer to prevent the pulp from becoming lumpy. Then pour a little of the mixture into a dish or bowl to make it easy to dip the strips of paper.

Dip the pieces of paper in the paste just before they are to be laid on the mould. You must make sure that you clean off any excess glue from the paper with your fingers before lay-

1

ing it in place. If you don't do this it will be difficult to make the surface smooth and even. Alternatively, use a brush to apply the glue to the pieces of paper.

If you have put too much paste on the surface, you can absorb the excess glue by laying some strips of dry paper on top. That way you will avoid bulges forming in the surface.

You can also soak the pieces of paper in the paste mix, but this makes it difficult to achieve a smooth surface. When you have applied the last layer of paper, smooth over the figure with your fingers. The surface will be fairly moist, so it is not difficult to even out any bumps.

When it comes to drying the models, you should allow about 2 days for them to be completely ready. It is important that they are thor-

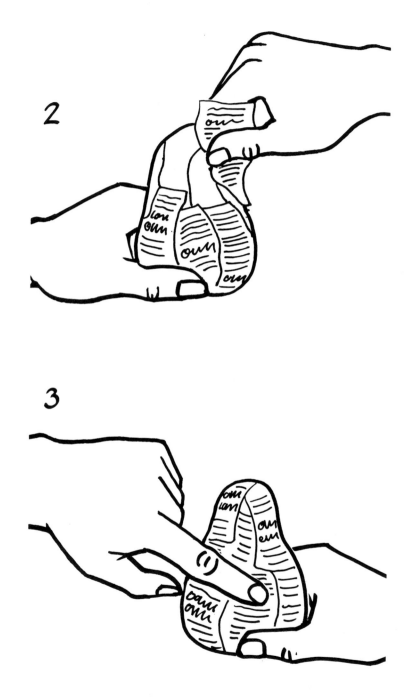

2

3

oughly dry before you remove the mould, otherwise they may fall to pieces. If you want to shorten the drying time, you can place the figures near to a radiator or in an airing-cupboard or use a hair-dryer. It is also important to make sure that the models are completely dry before you decorate them, otherwise the paint might crack (see page 18).

Instead of old newspaper you can use several other types of paper. One disadvantage of old newspaper is that, being very thin, you need several layers before the figure is ready. On the other hand, it is easier to smooth the surface if the paper is not too stiff.

With many of the models in this book white typing paper has been applied between the layers of newspaper. If you do this you will need fewer layers and the figure will be more durable. Another advantage with this method is that you can see how far you have covered because the layers look different. If you use only one type of paper, it can be difficult to judge whether or not you have managed to cover the figure with an equal thickness all round.

If you are happy to use old newspaper, you should allow 10–12 layers before the figure is ready. If you prefer to combine newspaper and typing paper, you need only apply 6–8 layers.

Remember that when you are modelling animals or other objects that have a large number of details, you will lose a little each time you apply a new layer. For that reason it might be advisable to use typing paper and newspaper.

PULP

Pulp is a mushy papier mâché mix, which is made from paper soaked in water with paste added. The pulp can be used for modelling in a variety of ways.

You can either construct solid figures — see the Punch and Judy puppets on page 63, for example — or shape the mass around a solid object such as a ball. In this way you can produce dishes or small bowls.

The pulp takes a fairly long time to dry, espe-cially if the figures are solid, and you should allow 4–5 days. However, even though this method requires a longer drying period than the strips of paper, it is still easier to carry out. It does not take a very long time to model a bowl or mould a figure, so this is something smaller children can get involved in. It is better to use old newspaper for the preparation, but remember that you will need to use plenty of paper if you are planning any large-scale projects.

Tear the paper into small squares, roughly 2 × 2cm (¾ × ¾in), place the pieces in a bowl or bucket and pour over boiling water until it just covers them. Now allow the paper to soak for about 3 hours, then whisk the mass with a hand-mixer until it has an even consistency. When the mixture is smooth, squeeze the pulp and remove all excess water. Next, make some cold-water paste, making a fairly stiff mixture, and whisk it into the paper mix. The pulp is ready when it seems solid but is still smooth. If you are using the pulp to make bowls, it must not be too thin, otherwise it may not hold together when you apply it to the mould. This is also the case if you are using it to make figures. If you follow these directions for making pulp you will have a versatile, workable substance. However, it is very difficult to achieve an even surface. So, if you want a smooth, uniform surface, follow the directions below.

If you prefer your models to have a smooth surface, you can add general-purpose filler, which makes the figures more robust. This comes in powder form and needs to be mixed with water. It is available from your local D-I-Y store. If you want to use this method, you should add equal parts of filler and paste — that is, half of the paste should be replaced with the filler mix. You can make a suitable mixture from half a bucket of newspaper and water with 1 cup of filler and 1 cup of paste.

When the models are dry, they can be brushed with a mixture of filler and water — the mixing proportions will be given on the packet — and you should use a large, soft brush. You can smooth off any bristle imprints left by the brush with a damp finger. After 3–4 hours you can sandpaper the model, but make sure that the sandpaper is not too coarse. If you are careful with the sandpapering, you can create a surface that looks almost as though the model has been made from clay. Remember too, that when you sandpaper you generate a great deal of dust. Therefore it is best to do this job outside or in a work room. General-purpose filler has been used for all the models in this book that have been made from pulp.

When you are working with the pulp it is a good idea to wear plastic gloves because the printer's ink comes off.

If you are going to be using a large amount of pulp, it is hardly worth making it yourself. You can buy pulp, which needs only to be mixed with water and it's ready for use, from some craft and hobby shops.

MOULDING

TORN PAPER

Papier mâché can be shaped around most solid objects. For example, the animals in this book have been modelled from plasticine and then covered with strips or pieces of papier mâché. It is not possible to lay the paper directly onto the plasticine because it will adhere to the dry model. To avoid this, cover the figure with kitchen film.

You can buy plasticine in 500g (1lb) packs from most good hobby shops. If the plasticine is too hard, it might be a good idea to put it inside a plastic bag and place this in warm water for 10–15 minutes. However, if you leave it for too long in warm water or if the weather is very hot, there is also a danger that it will become so soft that it is impossible to work with. If that happens, you can put it in the fridge for a few minutes. You can also soften plasticine by kneading it between your fingers. There are lots of different figures and objects that you can shape. Later in the book you will find a section giving details about modelling and the things you need to remember when you are ready to start.

When you have covered the model with strips of paper, it needs to dry. As soon as it is thoroughly dry, cut it with a craft knife to make two half shells. It is extremely important to make sure that it is completely dry, otherwise it will be very difficult to handle. Remove the former, then join the two halves once again using small strips of masking tape. If you make sure that the strips of tape are even, you can leave them in place under the subsequent layers. To conceal the join, cover the whole figure with one or two more layers of papier mâché. Add any loose details, such as the pear stalk, at the end, as shown in the illustrations on the opposite page.

The model itself can be used again if you wish, but you will need to cover it with a new layer of kitchen film as you cannot avoid damaging it when you split the papier mâché shell. It is more fun to make each figure a slightly different shape to the previous one so that you don't create two identical models.

You can also shape the models over an existing design, for example a bowl or a dish. Here, too, it is important to cover with film, and it is a good idea to smear the object with oil, otherwise it may be difficult to make the film stick.

In most cases it is easier to cover a bowl on the inside because it is a simple matter to lift the shell up out of the mould when it is dry. It is perfectly in order to let the papier mâché protrude over the top. As soon as it is dry you can trim it off with a craft knife.

It is also possible to shape models from corrugated card or smooth card and then cover these models with papier mâché. With this method you can make them as hard as wood or clay. The former should not be removed after it has been covered. The advantages of corrugated card are that it is flexible, easy to work with and does not crack. You can use it to create highly imaginative bowls and dishes. For solid rims you can use corrugated card from old cardboard boxes. If you are making objects with rims that are softer and easier to shape, you can use corrugated card in rolls, which you can buy at some stationers.

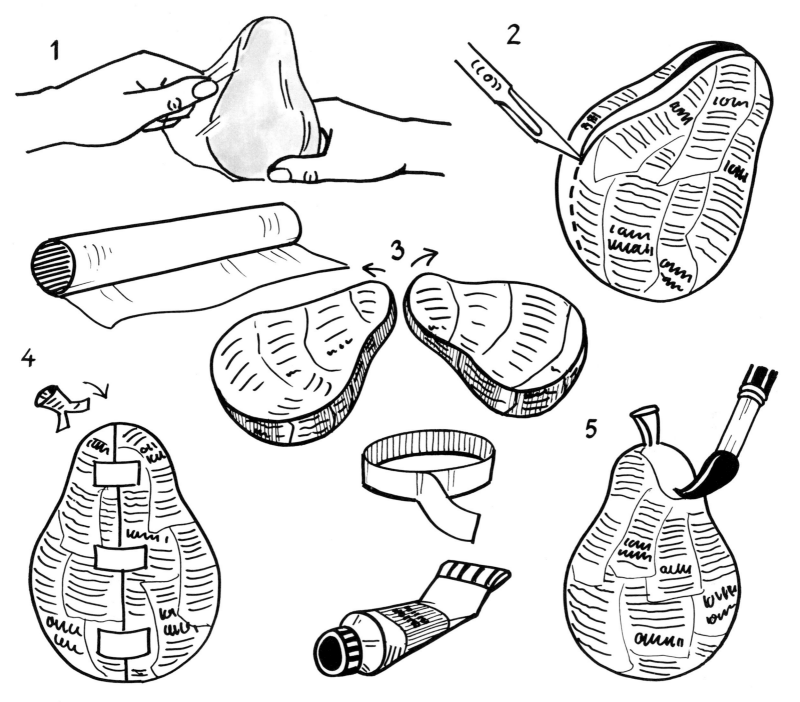

1

2

3

4

5

PULP

As mentioned earlier, pulp is a porridge-like mass that you can shape and mould into a large number of different objects. You will learn later how to shape the pulp into bowls and dishes, but this section is going to deal with moulding. The advantage with this method is that you can mass-produce the same figure once you have created the casting mould. It is important to use the filler and paste method described on page 13.

Shape the model that you want to mould in plasticine. Remember to make sure that it does not have too many details because these will be lost during the moulding process.

It is easier to mould models that do not have a "wrong" side — see, for example, the frames on page 66 — but it is also possible to make three-dimensional models. Shape the figure in plasticine. When it is ready, carefully cut it in two, making sure that it does not change shape. If that happens the two half sections may not fit together when they are cast. It is also extremely important to make sure that the cuts are clean.

Make the actual mould from plaster of Paris. For casting moulds you can use boxes or cartons such as shoe boxes. The advantage of boxes and cartons is that they can be torn up when the plaster of Paris is dry, which makes it easier to extract the mould. You should cover them on the inside with kitchen film. Grease the two half-figures carefully with petroleum jelly and place each one in its mould with the cut sides downwards. It is important to make sure that there is space all the way round — including over the figure, but it can also be a disadvantage if there is too much space because then you will

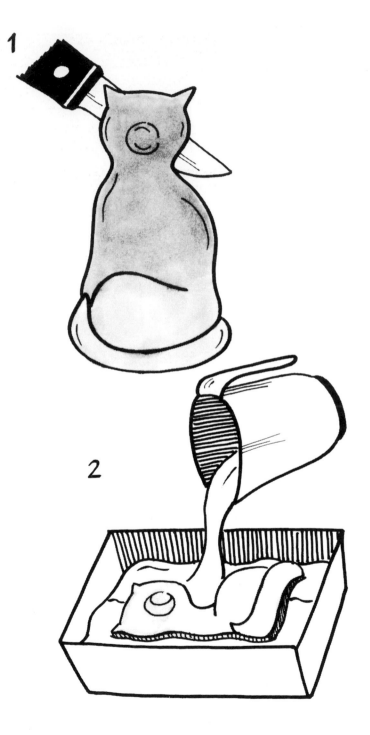

1

2

3

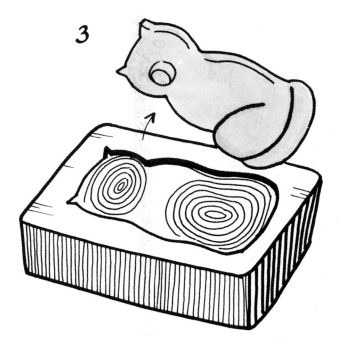

need to use a lot of plaster of Paris. Pour the plaster of Paris around the figure in the mould. There should be 3–5cm (1–2in) of plaster of Paris above the top edge of the figure.

While the plaster of Paris is hardening, it will become warm. It is only ready for use when it is completely cold, and it will be about 24 hours before you can use the mould. Remember that it is not possible to shorten the drying time by direct heat such as with a hair-dryer or on a radiator. All that will happen is that the plaster of Paris will crumble and the mould will be unusable. When the plaster of Paris is dry, you can free it from the box. Remove the kitchen film from the sides. If you have been careful in greasing the figure in petroleum jelly, it will not be difficult to remove it from the mould, but you may have to scrape it out with a spoon or a knife. Make sure that the mould is absolutely clean before you start the casting process, vacuum cleaning it if necessary.

Next, varnish the mould, which will make it easier to take out the figure. Pour pulp into the mould, pressing it so that it reaches all the corners. When the mould is full, the pulp should be completely level with the surface. Scrape off any excess pulp with a palette knife. As the pulp dries, it shrinks slightly so it is not too difficult to extract the mould. You can shorten the drying time by placing the mould on a radiator. It is dry when the figure will come easily out of the mould.

4

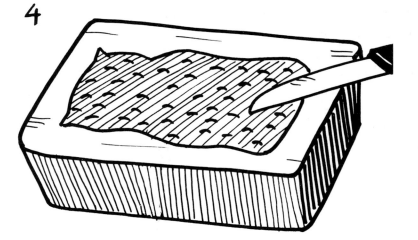

DECORATION

You will find that decorating the figure is the most exciting part of the work. If you want to achieve a really good result, it is worth taking your time.

PAINTING

Plastic paint and poster colours have been used for most of the models in this book. If other types of paint have been used, this is mentioned in the instructions for the models. Do not use oil-based paints as these are poisonous. Another disadvantage is that they take a long time to dry, and they sometimes shrink or crack when they are combined with paste.

It is well worth while priming the figures before you start. If you want to prevent the glue penetrating and causing discoloration, you can use a moisture-blocking, water-based paint for priming, which you can buy at your local D-I-Y store. Before you begin to decorate, it is very important to make sure that the model is completely dry. If it is not, the paint may crack because the papier mâché is a porous material, which is affected by fluctuations in temperature and humidity.

First of all you need to select the colours and patterns you want to use on the model. When you have primed the model, you can draw the pattern onto the surface with a pencil. If you use a soft pencil and draw lightly, it is easy to erase the marks afterwards when the model is decorated.

If you change your mind too often and paint too many layers on top of each other, the paint may crack. For that reason it is important not to make the paint too thick when you apply it. However, if you are not satisfied with the finished result, it is best to add a new layer of paper over the paint and begin again. It is advisable to let the model stand for 1–2 hours between each coat of paint so that the surface can dry thoroughly.

You can draw on small patterns and details with special water-based pens, which have great covering power. The ink comes out as you press the point against the base. The advantage of these pens is that they are easier to handle, especially for children. You can buy the pens in craft shops and from suppliers of artists' materials.

For large patterns you can use a brush to paint stripes, dots, rosettes and so on. To protect the surface you can varnish the models. It is extremely important to make sure that the varnish is water-based, otherwise there is the risk that the paint will crack.

PAPER

You can also create lots of stylish, abstract and imaginative patterns by applying coloured paper to the model as the final layer. For example, you can tear matt coloured paper into strips, squares or triangles and place these on the model. You will find a box made using this method illustrated on page 33. Here the pattern has been created by gluing strips of various colours onto the box. If you want a brighter surface, use glossy paper. Tissue paper can be used to create a special effect, particularly if you allow it to curl slightly when you apply it. You can also let the different colours overlap one another slightly so that they create as many shades as possible. However, do not apply too many layers of tissue paper, or you will lose the fine, transparent effect.

You can also achieve stunning effects by using patterned gift wrap. For example, you could cover the inside of a bowl with one pattern and use another pattern on the outside. You can also create a collage effect by using

pictures from periodicals and magazines. Another possibility is to use fragments of the pictures by tearing out sections that lie within a particular range of colours. Alternatively, you could draw your own pattern onto paper and glue it on. This method has been used for the bowl with roses that you can see illustrated on page 27. Here, a pattern of rose leaves has been drawn to cover the inside of the bowl.

OTHER MATERIALS

There are also many other decorative materials. For example, you could try experimenting with crepe paper, confetti, photocopied motifs, structured or patterned wallpaper or hand-made paper — the possibilities are practically unlimited.

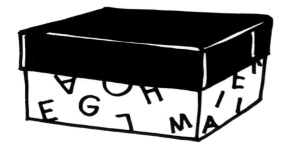

BOWLS

Bowls are very easy to make if you shape them around an existing model. Several different methods are explained in this section, and you can use papier mâché made from both paper and from pulp. It is easy to combine the bowls with each other to produce amusing designs. The bowls described first in this section have all been made from strips of paper.

BASIC BOWL MADE FROM TORN PAPER

This bowl is the basis of a number of the models in the book. It is very easy to make and is, therefore, an ideal project for less experienced people to start with.

Use an existing bowl or dish as a model. Line the model with strips of paper dipped in paste as described on page 10. It is up to you to decide whether to line the model on the outside or the inside but it is often easier to use the inside of the model as the paper will shrink slightly when drying. It is also easier to store

and move the bowl when it has been lined on the inside. Before lining the bowl, cover it with kitchen film, brushing the surface first with oil to make sure that the films sticks.

If the bowl is intended for everyday use, it is important to make sure that it is sturdy, so use 10–12 layers of paper for the lining. Allow each paper layer to dry a little before applying the next. Smooth out the layers and remove any excess glue to avoid bumps.

When you line the bowl, make sure that the strips reach slightly over the top of the rim. This makes it easier to free the bowl from the model when it is dry because there is an edge to grasp hold of. When the bowl is dry you can cut round the rim with a pair of scissors. You can either keep the rim curved or cut it away completely. If you want a thick rim, you can make a sausage shape out of pulp.

You can also expand the bowl — for example, by attaching a base as shown on page 24.

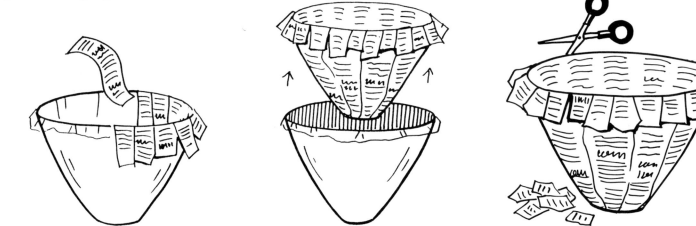

BOWL WITH BASE

First of all make the basic bowl as described on page 22. You can then give the bowl a base. It must be the right size so that the bowl does not fall over. You can combine several small bowls to make the base if you wish (see page 26).

If you want the bowl to be a centre-piece, you can use a paper cup as a model. One advantage of using a paper cup is that you do not need to apply so many layers of paper since the cup can become part of the model. You can buy paper cups in many different sizes.

If you want the base to have a slightly pointed shape, try using one of the conical-shaped spools you find with certain types of machine-knitting wool.

You can also make lots of usable models out of corrugated card. To make bases you could also use, for example, parts of an egg carton or a cardboard tube cut into sections. You could also make small bases out of pulp.

When you have lined the different parts, let them dry before you join them together with masking tape. After assembling the parts, line the whole model with a double layer of paper so that all the joins are invisible and the article appears to be a complete unit.

BOWLS MADE FROM SEVERAL PARTS

Begin by making the basic bowl as described on page 22. If you make several small bowls in the same way, you can place them together to form a base as in the illustration, although you will find that it is not possible to do this with all shapes. If the bowls are too high, there is a danger that the completed model may not stand up very well.

When the bowls are dry, you can tape them together with masking tape. Then cover them with one or two layers of paper so that all the joins are hidden.

Decoration

The illustration opposite shows a bowl made using this method. It has been adorned with papier mâché roses. You can find out how to make these roses on page 28.

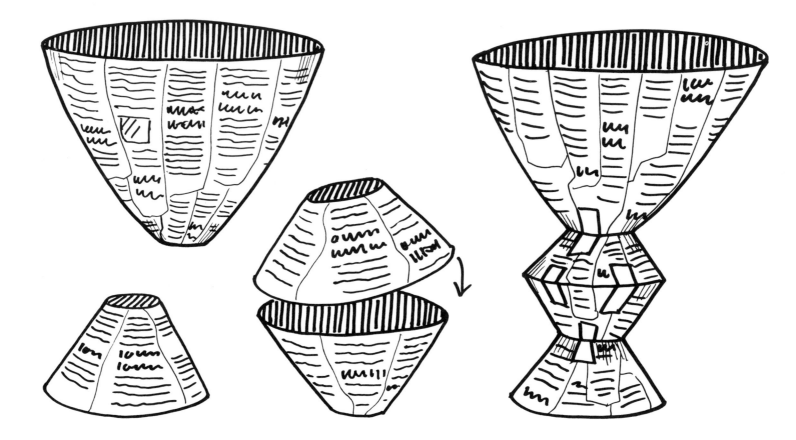

ROSES

The roses look very realistic even though they have been made from card. To make a medium-sized rose you will need 20–25 petals. Cut the petals from thin card, then leave them in paste for about half an hour. When they are saturated with paste, they are easy to shape.

Start by rolling a petal into the shape of a small tube. This will be the innermost petal in the flower. If you like, you can hold the petal in place with a thin strip of newspaper. Roll the next petal around the first but not too tightly. Continue in this way until most of the petals have been rolled around. Then, one by one, shape the petals so that they fold outwards like a rose in full bloom. Hold the petals together at the bottom with a thin strip of newspaper. Leave the rose to dry.

When you decorate the rose, it is best to use a spray paint so that you can reach inside all the hollows. Remember that it is dangerous to inhale spray paint so it is advisable to paint out of doors.

Six roses have been used for the bowl on page 27. Notches were cut around the rim for each rose to sit in, as shown in the illustration. If the rose has become too long during the modelling stage, you can cut away the bottom section. When the rose is sitting snugly in the notch, hold it securely in place with small pieces of paper.

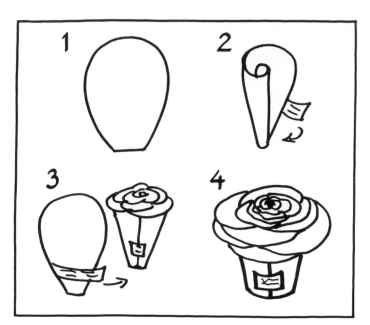

BASIC PULP BOWL

Pulp is a thick mass that is ideal for modelling. Ways of making it and guidelines on its use are given on pages 12–13. As mentioned earlier, you can also make a basic bowl from pulp. These bowls are more solid than those made from paper strips and are, therefore, longer lasting.

You can use a bowl or a dish for the basic mould. Cover this with kitchen film, and to ensure that the film will hold, brush the mould first with oil.

The pulp should not be too mushy or it may slip when it is pressed to the mould. To avoid such problems, it is best to cover the bowl on the inside. If you start from the base and work upwards it is fairly straightforward. You will also find it easier to create a smooth exterior when you cover the mould from the inside.

Instead of pressing the pulp, you can roll it out with a rolling pin. Place a piece of kitchen film on the table and lay the pulp on top. Place another piece of film on top of the pulp. Now you can roll out the pulp between the two layers. When the layer of pulp is even and smooth you can lift it over the mould between the two layers of film. You will find it easier if you have an assistant so that you can each look after one side. Now press on the pulp and remove the top section of film. If the pulp does not cover the inside of the bowl completely you can press it until it fits or roll out another piece. The layer of pulp should be about 1cm (½in) thick. Remove any excess pulp before leaving the model to dry.

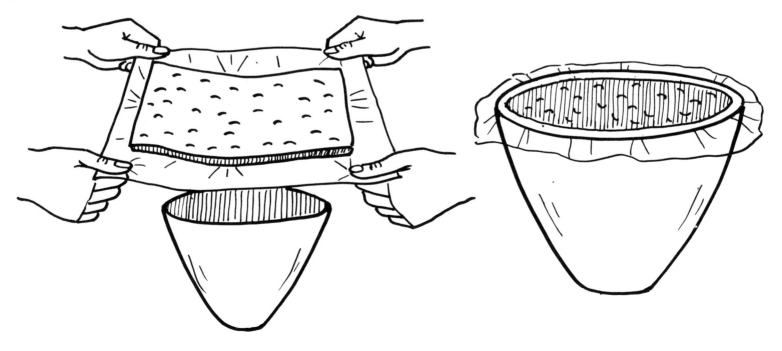

BOWL WITH CURVED RIM

First of all cover a high-sided bowl as explained on page 29. When the bowl is nearly dry, press the sides in towards the middle as shown in the illustration. It is important to make sure that the bowl is dry enough for the sides to stand on their own when they are pressed into shape.

Cracks can occur very easily in the bowl, but any that do appear can be repaired with soft pulp.

Decorating bowls

When the bowls are dry you can decorate them with soft pulp. For example, you can roll out sausage shapes or small balls and press them onto the side in an attractive pattern. You can also make attractive handles or bases to attach to the bowl.

On page 23 you will see a bowl that has been decorated as an orange with green leaves. The leaves are cut from card that has been attached to the rim of the bowl. After this they are covered with pulp that has been pressed on both sides of the leaves. You can make lots of imaginative decorations this way.

BOXES

All the boxes are made out of paper strips. There are many designs and models to choose from, and several of them are described in this section. You can also combine the different models to create entirely new designs. Most of the boxes are shaped around a card or corrugated card former. You will not be removing the card, so it is not necessary to use so many layers of paper.

ROUND BOX WITH LID

Use corrugated card to make the box. The base and lid should be the same size. If you like, use a disc or plate as a guide.

Measure the circumference of the circle and cut out a piece for the body. You should also have a rim for the lid. The two pieces should be exactly the same length as the circumference of the lid and base. Join the sides with masking tape.

When you have assembled the box, you need to make a rim, which you can tape inside at the top, to give the lid something to grip. This rim should have the same circumference as the inside of the box and should be about 6cm (2½in). high. Tape it in place so that half of it protrudes all the way round, as shown in the illustration.

To make a handle for the lid, cut a circle out of card. Snip a section in towards the middle and twist the circle like a flat cone until it looks like a small bowl, as in the illustration. Glue on the handle after you have covered it.

Decoration

The box on the opposite page has been decorated with strips of coloured paper. The paper has been torn into pieces and cut off at the top to form a white rim. The pieces are stuck on the box as a final layer of paper.

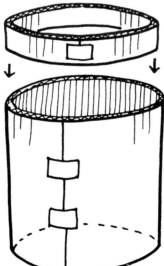
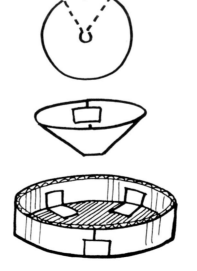

KIDNEY-SHAPED BOX

You can use the basic method on page 32 to make boxes with different shapes. The base and lid could, for example, be cut in a curve as shown in the illustration. You must make sure that they are identical so that the box and lid will match. Then cut the sides so that they match the lid and base. You could even make the handle curve the same way as the lid.

FRUIT BOXES

This box is shaped around a fruit, which is completely covered. A melon was used to make the box illustrated on page 39. It has been covered all the way round. As you can see, the stalk has also been covered. You should use 8–10 layers of paper.

When the papier mâché is completely dry, the mould should be cut around the centre with a craft knife. After you have cut through the model, glue a strip of card all the way round the inside of the upper edge. This strip will ensure that the lid sits perfectly in place.

Finally, the box in the illustration was covered with tissue paper to give it a translucent appearance. It doesn't matter if the paper curls slightly.

You can use several different fruits as moulds. However, it is important not to use fruit that is too soft. The best fruits are those that have a characteristic form.

You can also shape the model from plasticine. See page 38 for guideline on making different types of fruit from papier mâché.

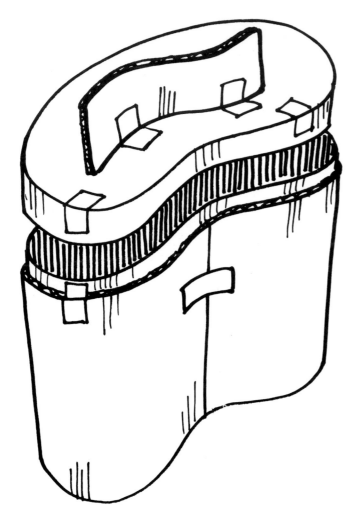

ANIMAL BOXES

By using a box for the basic form you can model an animal such as a duck. Start by cutting three oval pieces of corrugated card as shown in the illustration. Two of the ovals will be used for the lid and base. Make a rim from corrugated card to fit all the way round the lid. This should be about 1cm (½in) high and held in place with masking tape. The side, which is attached to the base sheet, should be about 5cm (2in) high depending upon the size of the box. Glue a thin strip inside the box along the rim all the way round to help to keep the lid in place.

The third sheet should be used as the base of the model for the body of the animal. It is important that the sides of the body are exactly in line with the shape of the sheet all the way round. Mould the model from plasticine, then cover it with 10–12 layers of paper. When it is dry, cut and assemble it as explained on pages 46–47. You will not be able to use the base sheet again as it goes soft after being in contact with the plasticine. Tape the model to the lid. Cover the

model and lid with one or two layers of paper to hide the connection between body and lid.

You can make lots of models that are suitable for boxes — a hen, a peacock, a hedgehog — or how about a ladybird?

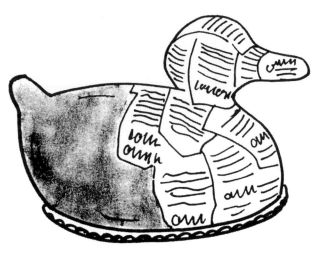

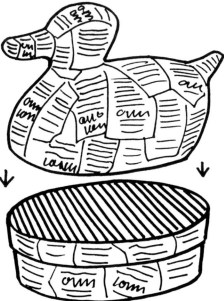

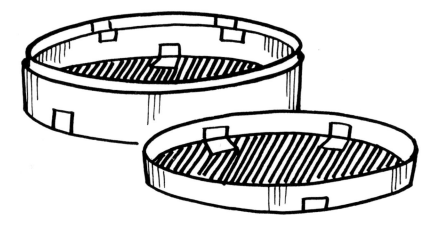

FRUITS

Fruits made from papier mâché make excellent decorative objects. They do not take very long to make and are easy to model. If you choose fruits that are not too soft, you can use the fruit itself for the mould. But I don't recommend that you eat the fruit afterwards! If you model the fruits from plasticine, use real fruits to copy from. Be sure to include all the details so that you make them as realistic as possible.

Cover the fruits with small pieces of paper. You will need to use 8–10 layers in order to preserve the shape. Apple and pear stalks can look a little awkward if you try to model them, so you may prefer to use a real stalk and glue it in position. The dried flower can be cut from green paper and glued to the other end. The onions should have a little tuft at the bottom. One way of making this is from strands of frayed rope. Insert the rope into a small hole and fasten it with glue.

You can make small leaves out of card which you glue on and cover with papier mâché. If you want to preserve the illusion that the fruits are real, don't make the leaves too heavy.

You can also make bread and rolls as shown in the picture opposite. Bread can be used for display, but I think that the fruits are more decorative. Mould the different types of bread in plasticine. If you make small pretzels, you can use them as Christmas decorations.

Decoration

The fruits in the picture opposite have been decorated with a layer of tissue paper in various colours. By tearing the paper into patterns you can achieve a shimmering effect. Some of the fruits have been painted on top of the tissue paper.

The fruits have been given a coat of clear varnish to make them shine.

Page 34 gives directions on how you can use the fruits to make boxes with lids.

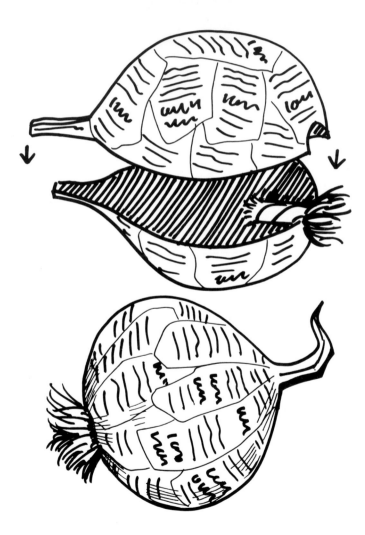

MASKS

Venice in Italy is well-known for the beautiful papier mâché masks that are used in the annual carnival. You will find lots of shops in the small streets between the canals that produce imaginative masks and sell them as souvenirs. Papier mâché masks are also made in China but in a very different way from the Venetian ones. The Chinese generally make masks that resemble animals or imaginary beings.

This section will show you how to make masks in two different ways. The first method involves making a framework of card and covering it with papier mâché strips. The second method involves modelling.

MASK SHAPED OVER A FRAMEWORK

The circumference and shape of the mask are determined by a strip of card stapled together to form a rim. Shape the actual profile by using another strip and attaching it as shown in the illustration. You could use soft curves or if you prefer make a point by bending the card. You should also make cross-pieces out of card. You can roll large balls of newspaper and place them under the mask so that the papier mâché does not collapse between the cross-pieces. Remove the paper balls when the mask is dry. If you like, you can make other stiffeners as you go along. See, for example, the cardboard sheet in the fish's mouth in the illustration.

When you have completed the whole framework, the mask should be covered with 10–12

layers of paper. Eyebrows, lips and other facial features can be modelled by shaping soaked newspaper and attaching it to the mask. Then apply several layers of paper on top of the features to keep the outline smooth.

You can also cut different sections in card and glue them to the mask — see the fins on the imaginary fish in the illustration, for example. The card sections should be covered with papier mâché.

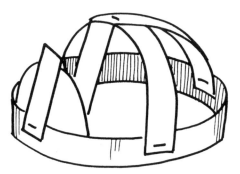

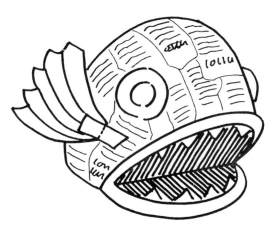

MODELLED MASK

If you want to make a mask with lots of details and a realistic appearance, it is best to mould it over plasticine.

Mould the mask from the plasticine and lay it on a sheet. It is advisable to cover the sheet with kitchen film to stop the plasticine getting stuck, and cover the mask with film as well.

Place 10–12 layers of paper over the mould. It is best to let the paper protrude slightly over the sheet so that there is an edge all round. When it is dry you can use this edge to glue a mane for a lion mask, for example (see the illustration). It is also ideal for attaching ears and other details.

Cut the lion's mane from pieces of card as shown in the illustration. The number of pieces will depend on the size of the mask. Cover the pieces with one or two layers of paper and glue them all round the edge. The bottom corners should just touch each other as shown.

Make the lion's teeth from pulp and press them into the mouth. Finally attach a stick to the mask so that you can hold it up in front of your face. If you prefer you can leave out the stick and attach a cord so that you can hang it on the wall as a decoration.

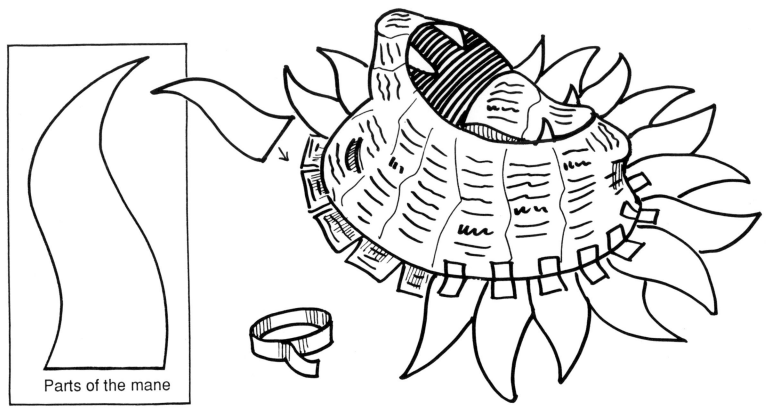

Parts of the mane

ANIMALS

Making animals out of papier mâché is especially enjoyable. It can take quite a long time to produce a model with lots of detail, but that doesn't make the work any the less exciting!

All the animals in this section have been moulded in plasticine. After that they have been covered with 6–8 layers of papier mâché. The simplest models are the ones without legs, such as the penguin on page 50.

Instructions for modelling an animal with legs are given on pages 46–48. This basic model can be combined and varied to produce every possible kind of animal. On pages 49–60 are descriptions of some of the animals that have been illustrated. Once you have learned the basic principles and techniques, it is very easy to make other animals.

ANIMALS WITH LEGS

The model illustrated here is the pig that you can see in the picture on page 49. I have chosen to make the pig because it is the simplest model with legs.

Before you start to mould the animal, you might like to seek some inspiration in a book on animals so that you can be sure that the proportions are as accurate as possible. You can, of

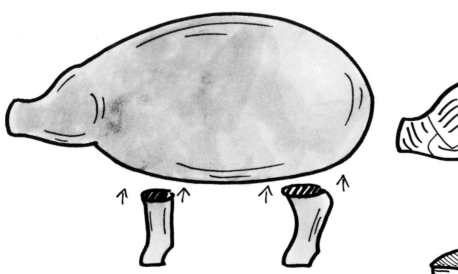

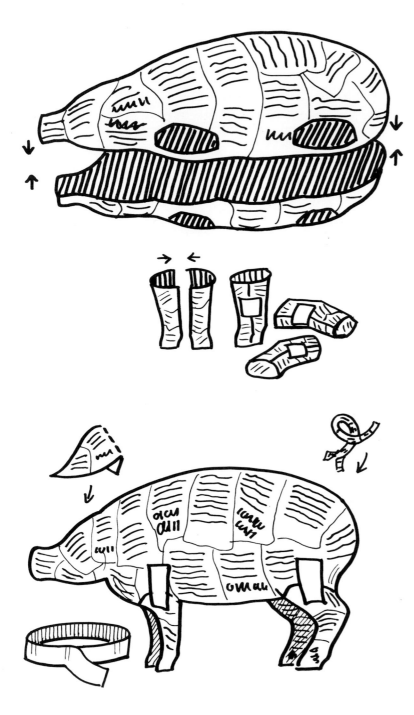

course, also achieve some splendid results by giving your imagination free rein.

Start by moulding the body and head in a single section. Do not model the small ears. Cut them from card and attach them at the very end. However, it is a good idea to try moulding a couple of ears in plasticine and fitting them loosely as this will give you an impression of how the head will look when the model is finished.

To make the legs, roll four small sausages and press them on to the body. The animal should be modelled in such a way that the joins are hidden. It is important to make sure that the model looks like a whole article and not an assembly of separate parts. For that reason you can only finish off the modelling when the legs are in place.

In many cases it is not possible to let the figure stand on its legs when it is covered in papier mâché. If the body is too heavy, the legs will be forced out of shape. It is sensible to cover the model when it is on its side. To help the model keep its shape you can lay it to dry on a soft base such as a towel with kitchen film over it.

When you have finished modelling the animal, it should be covered with strips of papier mâché. Make sure that you reach inside all the corners and smooth it out so as not to lose the small details. Then leave the model to dry.

When the model is completely dry, it should be carefully cut in two so that you can remove the plasticine. First cut the legs off, leaving a round section up on the body. It is a good idea to number the legs and their positions on the body so that you don't change them around when you come to reassemble them. Then cut the body lengthwise all the way round as shown in the illustration. Cut the legs in the same way and mark the pairs.

Use masking tape to hold the body pieces in position when you reassemble them. Assemble the body and legs separately and cover them with a layer of papier mâché.

When the parts are dry, fasten the legs to the body with masking tape. Cover the whole figure with a layer of papier mâché and leave to dry.

Finally attach the loose parts, in this case the ears and tail. Cut the ears from card and glue them in place. Make the tail from a piece of pipe cleaner covered in soaked newspaper. Cover the ears and the join at the tail with paper. Finally paint the figure.

PENGUIN

The penguin is fairly easy to make as it doesn't have any legs. The same applies to the seal shown in the picture on page 51.

Shape the body as shown in the illustration and cover it with papier mâché. Cut the flippers, feet, tail and beak out of card. The illustration shows the different sections more clearly. Line all parts with a double layer of papier mâché before you attach them. The beak should be thicker, so use more layers of paper here. Attach all the parts as shown and then cover the penguin with one more layer of paper to conceal the section between flippers and beak.

You can make the penguins in lots of different shapes as you can see from the illustration.

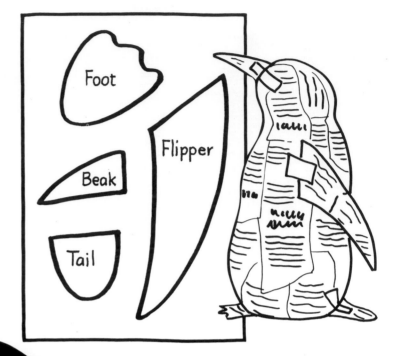

50

SNAKE

The snake is as easy to make as the penguin. Start by rolling a long sausage of plasticine. You can mould the sausage in any way you like. One end is going to form the head, and you should add a little extra plasticine round the strip. Press the mouth into shape as shown.

If you want to make a long, thick snake with its head raised as shown in the illustration, you will have to make it in several parts.

The snake in the illustration has been divided into three sections. You must be especially careful that the sections are uniformly thick when you cover them with papier mâché, otherwise it will be impossible to hide the joins afterwards.

Cover the plasticine sections with papier mâché. The end with the raised head should be laid on its side while you work, otherwise it will crumple.

When the papier mâché is dry, cut the sections through and remove the plasticine. Reassemble the parts, holding them together with masking tape, and apply a layer of papier mâché all around.

Make the tongue from a bent piece of pipe cleaner bent into a V. Cover it with soaked newspaper before setting it in place.

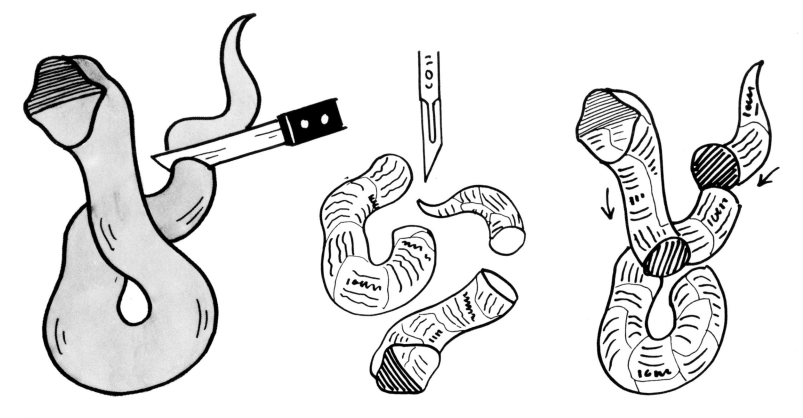

52

PARROT

Parrots make beautiful decorative objects. You can hang them from the ceiling or make them sit in a green plant.

Mould the body from plasticine as shown and cover it with 6–8 layers of paper. After you have covered, separated and reassembled the model, cut two wings and a long tail feather out of card. Each of the wings consists of one large section of card and a number of smaller, loose pieces as shown in the illustration. Cover the small pieces with 1–2 layers of paper before gluing them on. Attach the wings on either side of the body and cover the joins with a few layers of paper. The tail is an oblong strip of card folded along the dotted lines shown in the illustration. Cover the tail too with 1–2 layers of papier mâché before gluing it in place.

When the parrot is ready, decorate it in bright colours.

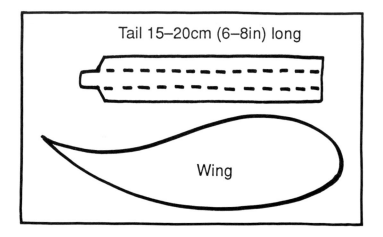

Tail 15–20cm (6–8in) long

Wing

54

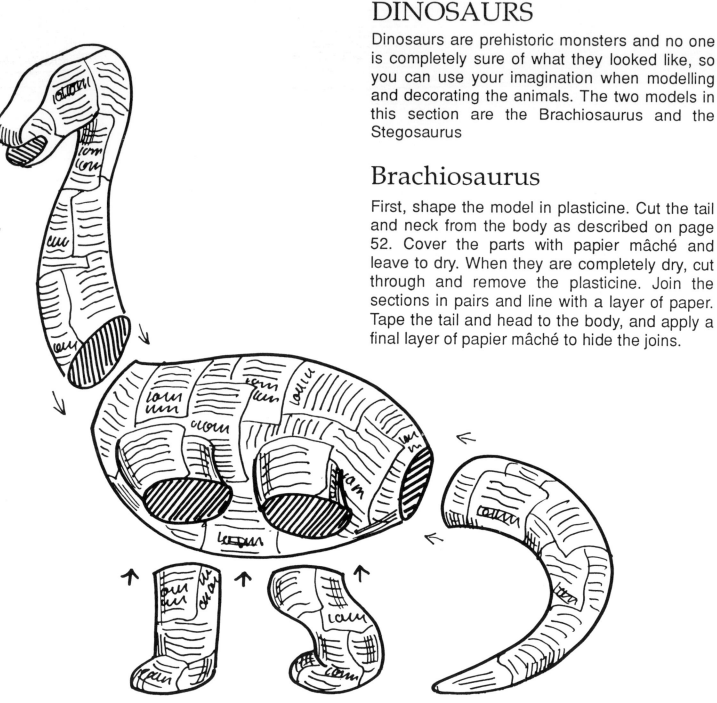

DINOSAURS

Dinosaurs are prehistoric monsters and no one is completely sure of what they looked like, so you can use your imagination when modelling and decorating the animals. The two models in this section are the Brachiosaurus and the Stegosaurus

Brachiosaurus

First, shape the model in plasticine. Cut the tail and neck from the body as described on page 52. Cover the parts with papier mâché and leave to dry. When they are completely dry, cut through and remove the plasticine. Join the sections in pairs and line with a layer of paper. Tape the tail and head to the body, and apply a final layer of papier mâché to hide the joins.

Stegosaurus

Shape the model in plasticine. Because of the length and shape of the tail, it should be cut off at the root before it is covered. If you like, you can do this with the head as well.

After you have covered, separated and reassembled the model, cut the spines that run down the back out of card. These pieces are largest in the middle of the creature and become smaller towards the head and towards the tail as shown in the illustration. The number you attach depends upon the size of the stegosaurus. The model shown on page 57 has 24 pieces. Cover the pieces with 1–2 layers of paper and attach them along the back with masking tape.

The spikes on the tail are made from twists of paper covered with papier mâché. Fit them to the tail in the same way as the spines on the back. Cover the whole figure with another layer of papier mâché to conceal all joins, and then decorate it.

Back pieces

PUPPETS

You can create lots of beautiful puppets out of papier mâché. It is possible to make puppets with a body, arms and legs, as explained in the instructions for making the bear on pages 64–65. This method will allow you to shape the different sections around plasticine to make them hollow. You can decorate the body, arms and legs so that it looks as though the puppet has clothes on.

Alternatively, you could model the head, hands and feet out of pulp and sew them to a fabric body as with the old porcelain dolls. The puppets can make a fine impression if you take some trouble over the decoration.

The puppets shown on page 63 represent Punch and Judy. Papier mâché is ideal for making puppets because it is so light. Heads made from clay or wood are heavier and therefore more difficult to handle.

Model the head out of pulp and sew it to the body. You can either mould the hands and feet from pulp too or make them out of felt. There is a very simple pattern on page 62 that you can use for a puppet without legs. The pattern has been drawn half-size. The size is suitable for the head described below.

Modelling the head

Model the head around a cardboard tube that is 5–6cm (2–2½in) long and about 2cm (¾in) in diameter. You can roll the tube out of card and hold it together with masking tape. If you like you can roll the tube so that it forms a slight point at the end — almost like a cone. The tube is for you to put your fingers inside when you come to perform with the puppet.

Roll soaked strips of newspaper around the tube so that it is thickest in the middle. In place of newspaper you can use tin foil which is also light and easy to shape. Push the tube down into a bottle so that you have both hands free while you work.

Model the head from pulp, which you should press around the tube. In the beginning it should look something like a large egg, 10–12cm (4–5in) long and 7–8cm (3–3½in) wide. Continue to shape the neck around the tube in this way. It is important that the tube is covered all the way round.

Mould the ears, nose and chin by adding a little extra pulp. Shape the cheeks, eye sockets, nostrils and mouth with a modelling tool or a small, blunt knife.

If you want the figure to appear close-cropped you can use a darning needle for the hair and eyebrows. The best time to do this is when the figure is half-dry. If you prefer, you can cut hair from thin yarn and glue it on after the head has been decorated.

After you have decorated the head, leave it to dry. Then you can paint it.

Finally, sew the head to the body, gathering the material around the neck. To stop the head from falling off you can add some glue to the neck before you gather the material in position.

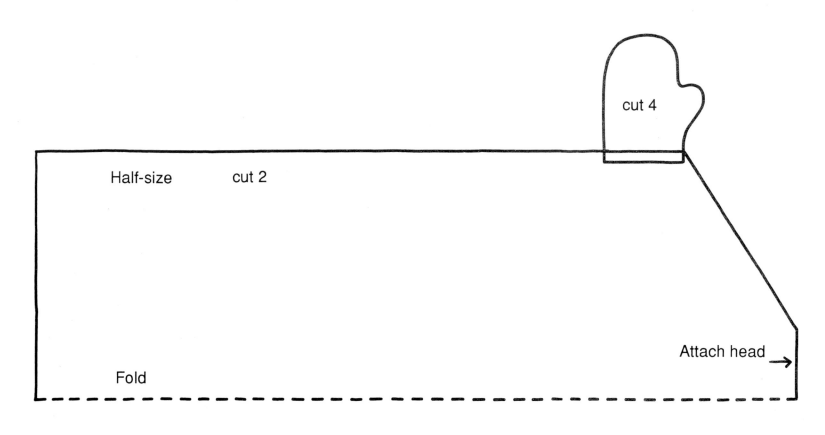

cut 4

Half-size   cut 2

Fold

Attach head →

BEAR

This bear looks like a real, old-fashioned teddy bear. It consists of a body with a head, two arms and two legs.

Start by modelling the head. The nose should protrude a little, as you can see in the illustration. The ears should not be modelled but made from card and added at the end.

Shape the body until it looks something like an oblong egg. Attach the head to the body and smooth over the join. The neck should be fairly thick.

Model the arms and legs from plasticine sausages. They should be almost the same length. Bend the feet upwards slightly and press the soles flat. Do the same with the paws on the side facing in towards the body.

Cover the different parts with paper. Cut the ears from card as shown in the illustration. Glue

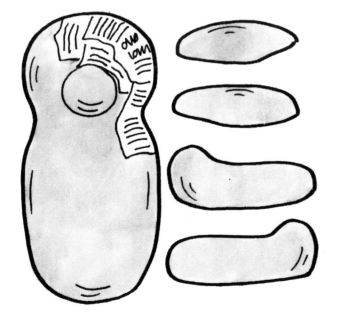

them in place on the head and cover them with 3–4 layers of paper. Leave the various pieces to dry.

Decoration

Paint the body, arms and legs yellow. The paws and the soles of the feet should be dark brown or black. Paint the nose and eyes on as shown. If you like you can use a felt-tipped pen.

Use a strong darning needle to make holes through the body, arms and legs so that the sections can be joined with round elastic. Tie knots at the ends of the elastic.

Instead of a bear you could make a doll in the same way. You could paint this to make it look as though it was wearing clothes, or make some clothes for it.

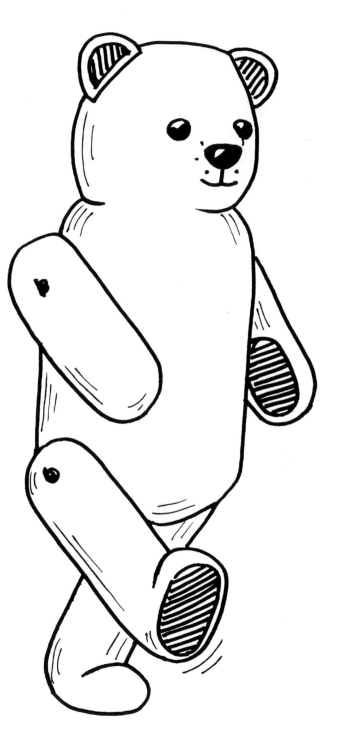

FRAMES

The frames are made from pulp that has been cast-moulded as explained on pages 16–17. The frames in the picture opposite are rectangular, but obviously you can make them in any shapes you like.

The frames are ideal for mirrors. After they have been moulded you can decorate them if you wish. You could apply decorative patterns of pulp or you could roll strips or make other shapes from the pulp and press them on to the frame as ornaments.

When the frames are dry you can paint them with poster colours and then varnish. Gold bronze on mirror frames gives them an antique appearance. You can actually mould the pulp in such a way as to make it look as if the frame were made of old, slightly decaying wood.

You can also make small figures and glue them on top of the frame as shown in the picture opposite. These figures can either be cast-moulded or shaped in pulp.

When the frame is finished, fit the glass and backing board into position.

A CIP catalogue record for this book is
available from the British Library.

Published by David Porteous
P.O. Box 5
Chudleigh
Newton Abbot
Devon TQ13 0YZ

ISBN 1 870586 09 3

Danish edition © 1991 Forlaget Klematis:
Pap Maché

English edition © 1993 David Porteous

Translated by Tim Bowler.

Printed in Hong Kong.